~~The weather
Overcast
Rain Imminent~~

LAUREN.MCKINLAY@EVANS

HALSHAW.COM

PEAKY BLINDERS
& RACECOURSE VILLAINS

A Rogues Gallery of Birmingham Peakies

NOSTALGIC NOTEBOOK

MAP SHOWING THE SMALL HEATH AREA OF BIRMINGHAM C1890, WHERE THE PEAKY BLINDER GANG EMINATED
Deritend
Small Heath
BORDESLEY
Camp Hill
Goods Sta.
Engine Ho.
R. Rea
MIDLAND WORKS
GAS WORKS
COLEMAN STREET
Small Arms Factory

VICTORIAN VIEW OF INDUSTRIAL BIRMINGHAM - BIRTHPLACE OF THE PEAKY BLINDERS

BIRMINGHAM LAW COURTS - CORPORATION STREET - ATTACHED VIA A TUNNEL TO THE LOCK-UP

PERSONAL NOTES

Name

Address

Telephone

Mobile

Email

In case of emergency please contact:

Name

Contact

Doctor

Doctor Telephone

Known Allergires

WEBSITES

~~[illegible]~~
~~[illegible]~~

(18) Pieck ~~[illegible]~~
Yamamoto

female
She/Her
Bicurious

November 17
2003

Ethnicity
~~Nationality~~: Asian
Nationality: Vietnameise
\+ Palestinian

CONTACTS

CONTACTS

BIRTHDAYS

January

1	17
2	18
3	19
4	20
5	21
6	22
7	23
8	24
9	25
10	26
11	27
12	28
13	29
14	30
15	31
16	

February

1	17
2	18
3	19
4	20
5	21
6	22
7	23
8	24
9	25
10	26
11	27
12	28
13	29
14	
15	
16	

March

1	17
2	18
3	19
4	20
5	21
6	22
7	23
8	24
9	25
10	26
11	27
12	28
13	29
14	30
15	31
16	

April

1	17
2	18
3	19
4	20
5	21
6	22
7	23
8	24
9	25
10	26
11	27
12	28
13	29
14	30
15	
16	

May

1	17
2	18
3	19
4	20
5	21
6	22
7	23
8	24
9	25
10	26
11	27
12	28
13	29
14	30
15	31
16	

June

1	17
2	18
3	19
4	20
5	21
6	22
7	23
8	24
9	25
10	26
11	27
12	28
13	29
14	30
15	
16	

BIRTHDAYS

July

1	17
2	18
3	19
4	20
5	21
6	22
7	23
8	24
9	25
10	26
11	27
12	28
13	29
14	30
15	31
16	

August

1	17
2	18
3	19
4	20
5	21
6	22
7	23
8	24
9	25
10	26
11	27
12	28
13	29
14	30
15	31
16	

September

1	17
2	18
3	19
4	20
5	21
6	22
7	23
8	24
9	25
10	26
11	27
12	28
13	29
14	30
15	
16	

October

1	17
2	18
3	19
4	20
5	21
6	22
7	23
8	24
9	25
10	26
11	27
12	28
13	29
14	30
15	31
16	

November

1	17
2	18
3	19
4	20
5	21
6	22
7	23
8	24
9	25
10	26
11	27
12	28
13	29
14	30
15	
16	

December

1	17
2	18
3	19
4	20
5	21
6	22
7	23
8	24
9	25
10	26
11	27
12	28
13	29
14	30
15	31
16	

2018

January

WK	M	T	W	T	F	S	S
1	1	2	3	4	5	**6**	**7**
2	8	9	10	11	12	**13**	**14**
3	15	16	17	18	19	**20**	**21**
4	22	23	24	25	26	**27**	**28**
5	29	30	31				

February

WK	M	T	W	T	F	S	S
5				1	2	**3**	**4**
6	5	6	7	8	9	**10**	**11**
7	12	13	14	15	16	**17**	**18**
8	19	20	21	22	23	**24**	**25**
9	26	27	28				

March

WK	M	T	W	T	F	S	S
9				1	2	**3**	**4**
10	5	6	7	8	9	**10**	**11**
11	12	13	14	15	16	**17**	**18**
12	19	20	21	22	23	**24**	**25**
13	26	27	28	29	30	**31**	

April

WK	M	T	W	T	F	S	S
13							**1**
14	2	3	4	5	6	**7**	**8**
15	9	10	11	12	13	**14**	**15**
16	16	17	18	19	20	**21**	**22**
17	23	24	25	26	27	**28**	**29**
18	30						

May

WK	M	T	W	T	F	S	S
18		1	2	3	4	**5**	**6**
19	7	8	9	10	11	**12**	**13**
20	14	15	16	17	18	**19**	**20**
21	21	22	23	24	25	**26**	**27**
22	28	29	30	31			

June

WK	M	T	W	T	F	S	S
22					1	**2**	**3**
23	4	5	6	7	8	**9**	**10**
24	11	12	13	14	15	**16**	**17**
25	18	19	20	21	22	**23**	**24**
26	25	26	27	28	29	**30**	

July

WK	M	T	W	T	F	S	S
26							**1**
27	2	3	4	5	6	**7**	**8**
28	9	10	11	12	13	**14**	**15**
29	16	17	18	19	20	**21**	**22**
30	23	24	25	26	27	**28**	**29**
31	30	31					

August

WK	M	T	W	T	F	S	S
31			1	2	3	**4**	**5**
32	6	7	8	9	10	**11**	**12**
33	13	14	15	16	17	**18**	**19**
34	20	21	22	23	24	**25**	**26**
35	27	28	29	30	31		

September

WK	M	T	W	T	F	S	S
35						**1**	**2**
36	3	4	5	6	7	**8**	**9**
37	10	11	12	13	14	**15**	**16**
38	17	18	19	20	21	**22**	**23**
39	24	25	26	27	28	**29**	**30**

October

WK	M	T	W	T	F	S	S
40	1	2	3	4	5	**6**	**7**
41	8	9	10	11	12	**13**	**14**
42	15	16	17	18	19	**20**	**21**
43	22	23	24	25	26	**27**	**28**
44	29	30	31				

November

WK	M	T	W	T	F	S	S
44				1	2	**3**	**4**
45	5	6	7	8	9	**10**	**11**
46	12	13	14	15	16	**17**	**18**
47	19	20	21	22	23	**24**	**25**
48	26	27	28	29	30		

December

WK	M	T	W	T	F	S	S
48						**1**	**2**
49	3	4	5	6	7	**8**	**9**
50	10	11	12	13	14	**15**	**16**
51	17	18	19	20	21	**22**	**23**
52	24	25	26	27	28	**29**	**30**
1							

2019

January

WK	M	T	W	T	F	S	S
1		1	2	3	4	**5**	**6**
2	7	8	9	10	11	**12**	**13**
3	14	15	16	17	18	**19**	**20**
4	21	22	23	24	25	**26**	**27**
5	28	29	30	31			

February

WK	M	T	W	T	F	S	S
5					1	**2**	**3**
6	4	5	6	7	8	**9**	**10**
7	11	12	13	14	15	**16**	**17**
8	18	19	20	21	22	**23**	**24**
9	25	26	27	28	29	**30**	

March

WK	M	T	W	T	F	S	S
9					1	**2**	**3**
10	4	5	6	7	8	**9**	**10**
11	11	12	13	14	15	**16**	**17**
12	18	19	20	21	22	**23**	**24**
13	25	26	27	28	29	**30**	**31**

April

WK	M	T	W	T	F	S	S
14	1	2	3	4	5	**6**	**7**
15	8	9	10	11	12	**13**	**14**
16	15	16	17	18	19	**20**	**21**
17	22	23	24	25	26	**27**	**28**
18	29	30					

May

WK	M	T	W	T	F	S	S
18			1	2	3	4	5
19	6	7	8	9	10	**11**	**12**
20	13	14	15	16	17	**18**	**19**
21	20	21	22	23	24	**25**	**26**
22	27	28	29	30	31		

June

WK	M	T	W	T	F	S	S
22						**1**	**2**
23	3	4	5	6	7	**8**	**9**
24	10	11	12	13	14	**15**	**16**
25	17	18	19	20	21	**22**	**23**
26	24	25	26	27	28	**29**	**30**

July

WK	M	T	W	T	F	S	S
27	1	2	3	4	5	**6**	**7**
28	8	9	10	11	12	**13**	**14**
29	15	16	17	18	19	**20**	**21**
30	22	23	24	25	26	**27**	**28**
31	29	30	31				

August

WK	M	T	W	T	F	S	S
31				1	2	**3**	**4**
32	5	6	7	8	9	**10**	**11**
33	12	13	14	15	16	**17**	**18**
34	19	20	21	22	23	**24**	**25**
35	26	27	28	29	30	**31**	

September

WK	M	T	W	T	F	S	S
35							**1**
36	2	3	4	5	6	**7**	**8**
37	9	10	11	12	13	**14**	**15**
38	16	17	18	19	20	**21**	**22**
39	23	24	25	26	27	**28**	**29**
40	30						

October

WK	M	T	W	T	F	S	S
40		1	2	3	4	**5**	**6**
41	7	8	9	10	11	**12**	**13**
42	14	15	16	17	18	**19**	**20**
43	21	22	23	24	25	**26**	**27**
44	28	29	30	31			

November

WK	M	T	W	T	F	S	S
44					1	2	3
45	4	5	6	7	8	**9**	**10**
46	11	12	13	14	15	**16**	**17**
47	18	19	20	21	22	**23**	**24**
48	25	26	27	28	29	**30**	

December

WK	M	T	W	T	F	S	S
48							**1**
49	2	3	4	5	6	**7**	**8**
50	9	10	11	12	13	**14**	**15**
51	16	17	18	19	20	**21**	**22**
52	23	24	25	26	27	**28**	**29**
1	30	31					

2020

January

WK	M	T	W	T	F	S	S
1			1	2	3	**4**	**5**
2	6	7	8	9	10	**11**	**12**
3	13	14	15	16	17	**18**	**19**
4	20	21	22	23	24	**25**	**26**
5	27	28	29	30	31		

February

WK	M	T	W	T	F	S	S
5						**1**	**2**
6	3	4	5	6	7	**8**	**9**
7	10	11	12	13	14	**15**	**16**
8	17	18	19	20	21	**22**	**23**
9	24	25	26	27	28	**29**	

March

WK	M	T	W	T	F	S	S
9							**1**
10	2	3	4	5	6	**7**	**8**
11	9	10	11	12	13	**14**	**15**
12	16	17	18	19	20	**21**	**22**
13	23	24	25	26	27	**28**	**29**
14	30	31					

April

WK	M	T	W	T	F	S	S
14			1	2	3	**4**	**5**
15	6	7	8	9	10	**11**	**12**
16	13	14	15	16	17	**18**	**19**
17	20	21	22	23	24	**25**	**26**
18	27	28	29	30	31		

May

WK	M	T	W	T	F	S	S
18					1	**2**	**3**
19	4	5	6	7	8	**9**	**10**
20	11	12	13	14	15	**16**	**17**
21	18	19	20	21	22	**23**	**24**
22	25	26	27	28	29	**30**	**31**

June

WK	M	T	W	T	F	S	S
23	1	2	3	4	5	**6**	**7**
24	8	9	10	11	12	**13**	**14**
25	15	16	17	18	19	**20**	**21**
26	22	23	24	25	26	**27**	**28**
27	29	30					

July

WK	M	T	W	T	F	S	S
27			1	2	3	**4**	**5**
28	6	7	8	9	10	**11**	**12**
29	13	14	15	16	17	**18**	**19**
30	20	21	22	23	24	**25**	**26**
31	27	28	29	30	31		

August

WK	M	T	W	T	F	S	S
31						**1**	**2**
32	3	4	5	6	7	**8**	**9**
33	10	11	12	13	14	**15**	**16**
34	17	18	19	20	21	**22**	**23**
35	24	25	26	27	28	**29**	**30**
36	31						

September

WK	M	T	W	T	F	S	S
36		1	2	3	4	**5**	**6**
37	7	8	9	10	11	**12**	**13**
38	14	15	16	17	18	**19**	**20**
39	21	22	23	24	25	**26**	**27**
40	28	29	30				

October

WK	M	T	W	T	F	S	S
40				1	2	**3**	**4**
41	5	6	7	8	9	**10**	**11**
42	12	13	14	15	16	**17**	**18**
43	19	20	21	22	23	**24**	**25**
44	26	27	28	29	30	**31**	

November

WK	M	T	W	T	F	S	S
44							**1**
45	2	3	4	5	6	**7**	**8**
46	9	10	11	12	13	**14**	**15**
47	16	17	18	19	20	**21**	**22**
48	23	24	25	26	27	**28**	**29**
49	30						

December

WK	M	T	W	T	F	S	S
49		1	2	3	4	**5**	**6**
50	7	8	9	10	11	**12**	**13**
51	14	15	16	17	18	**19**	**20**
52	21	22	23	24	25	**26**	**27**
53	28	29	30	31			

SUNRISE AND SUNSET

Times are for London and are in Greenwich Mean Time with British Summer Time allowed for.

July 2018

d	Rise h m	Set h m
7	04 52	21 18
14	04 59	21 13
21	05 08	21 05
28	05 18	20 55

October 2018

d	Rise h m	Set h m
6	07 09	18 28
13	07 21	18 12
20	07 33	17 57
27	07 45	17 43

January 2019

d	Rise h m	Set h m
5	08 05	16 07
12	08 02	16 16
19	07 56	16 27
26	07 48	16 43

April 2019

d	Rise h m	Set h m
6	06 25	19 42
13	06 10	19 54
20	05 55	20 05
27	05 41	20 17

August 2018

d	Rise h m	Set h m
4	05 28	20 44
11	05 39	20 31
18	05 50	20 18
25	06 02	20 03

November 2018

d	Rise h m	Set h m
3	06 57	16 31
10	07 09	16 19
17	07 22	16 09
24	07 33	16 01

February 2019

d	Rise h m	Set h m
2	07 38	16 52
9	07 26	17 05
16	07 13	17 17
23	06 59	17 30

May 2019

d	Rise h m	Set h m
6	05 27	20 29
13	05 15	20 40
20	05 05	20 50
27	04 56	21 00

September 2018

d	Rise h m	Set h m
1	06 13	19 48
8	06 24	19 32
15	06 35	19 16
22	06 46	19 00
29	06 58	18 43

December 2018

d	Rise h m	Set h m
1	07 43	15 56
8	07 52	15 52
15	07 59	15 52
22	08 04	15 55
29	08 06	16 00

March 2019

d	Rise h m	Set h m
2	06 44	17 42
9	06 29	17 55
16	06 13	18 07
23	05 57	18 19
30	05 41	18 30

June 2019

d	Rise h m	Set h m
1	04 49	21 08
8	04 45	21 15
15	04 43	21 20
22	04 43	21 22
29	04 46	21 22

METRIC CONVERSION TABLES

Bold figures equal units of either of the columns beside them: 1 cm - 0.394" and 1" = 2.540cm.

Centimetres		Inches	Metres		Yards	Kilometres		Miles	Square cm		Square in	Square m		Square yd
2.540	**1**	0.394	0.940	**1**	1.094	2.540	**1**	0.394	2.540	**1**	0.394	2.540	**1**	0.394
5.080	**2**	0.787	1.829	**2**	2.187	5.080	**2**	0.787	5.080	**2**	0.787	5.080	**2**	0.787
7.620	**3**	1.181	2.743	**3**	3.281	7.620	**3**	1.181	7.620	**3**	1.181	7.620	**3**	1.181
10.160	**4**	1.575	3.658	**4**	4.374	10.160	**4**	1.575	10.160	**4**	1.575	10.160	**4**	1.575
12.700	**5**	1.969	4.572	**5**	5.468	12.700	**5**	1.969	12.700	**5**	1.969	12.700	**5**	1.969
15.240	**6**	2.362	5.486	**6**	6.562	15.240	**6**	2.362	15.240	**6**	2.362	15.240	**6**	2.362
17.780	**7**	2.756	6.401	**7**	7.655	17.780	**7**	2.756	17.780	**7**	2.756	17.780	**7**	2.756
20.320	**8**	3.150	7.315	**8**	8.749	20.320	**8**	3.150	20.320	**8**	3.150	20.320	**8**	3.150
22.860	**9**	3.543	8.230	**9**	9.843	22.860	**9**	3.543	22.860	**9**	3.543	22.860	**9**	3.543

Cubic cm		Cubic in	Cubic m		Cubic yd	Litres		Gallons	Kilograms		Pounds	Metric tonnes		Tons(UK)
16.387	**1**	0.061	0.765	**1**	1.308	4.546	**1**	0.220	0.454	**1**	2.205	1.016	**1**	0.984
32.774	**2**	0.122	1.529	**2**	2.616	9.092	**2**	0.440	0.907	**2**	4.409	2.032	**2**	1.968
49.161	**3**	0.183	2.294	**3**	3.924	13.638	**3**	0.660	1.361	**3**	6.614	3.048	**3**	2.953
65.548	**4**	0.244	3.058	**4**	5.232	18.184	**4**	0.880	1.814	**4**	8.818	4.064	**4**	3.937
81.936	**5**	0.305	3.823	**5**	6.540	22.730	**5**	1.100	2.268	**5**	11.023	5.080	**5**	4.921
98.323	**6**	0.366	4.587	**6**	7.848	27.277	**6**	1.320	2.722	**6**	13.228	6.096	**6**	5.905
114.170	**7**	0.427	5.352	**7**	9.156	31.823	**7**	1.540	3.175	**7**	15.432	7.112	**7**	6.889
131.097	**8**	0.488	6.116	**8**	10.464	36.369	**8**	1.760	3.629	**8**	17.637	8.128	**8**	7.874
147.484	**9**	0.549	6.881	**9**	11.772	40.915	**9**	1.980	4.082	**9**	19.842	9.144	**9**	8.858

CONVERSION FACTORS

To convert to metric, multiply by the factor shown. To convert from metric, divide by the factor.

Length

miles: kilometres	1.6093
yards: metres	0.9144
feet: metres	0.3048
inches: millimetres	25.4
inches: centimetres	2.54

Volume

cubic yards: cubic metres	0.7646
cubic feet: cubic metres	0.0283
cubic inches: cubic centimetres	16.3871

Velocity

miles per hour: kilometres per hour	1.6093

Area

square miles: square kilometres	2.59
square miles: hectares	258.999
acres: square metres	4046.86
acres: hectares	0.4047
square yards: square metres	0.8361
square feet: square metres	0.0929
square feet: square centimetres	929.03
square inches: square millimetres	645.16
square inces: square centimetres	6.4516

Fuel Consumption

gallons per mile: litres per kilometre	2.825
miles per gallon: kilometres per litre	0.354

Mass

tons: kilograms	1016.05
tons: tonnes	1.0160
hundredweights: kilograms	50.8023
pounds: kilograms	0.4536
ounces: grams	28.3495

Capacity

gallons: cubic decimetres	4.5461
gallons: litres	4.546
US barrels: cubic metres (for petroleum)	0.159
pints: cubic decimetres	0.5683
pints: litres	0.568

NOTABLE DATES

UK and Republic of Ireland Holidays	2018	2019
New Year Holiday		
(UK, Rep. of Ireland)	Jan 1	Jan 1
Holiday (Scotland)	Jan 2	Jan 2
St. Patrick's Day (Rep. of Ireland)	Mar 17	Mar 17
Holiday (Nothern Ireland)	Mar 17	Mar 17
Good Friday (UK)	Mar 30	Apr 19
Easter Monday		
(UK, Rep. of Ireland)	Apr 2	Apr 22
May Day Holiday		
(UK, Rep. of Ireland)	May 7	May 6
Spring Holiday (UK)	May 28	May 27
Holiday (Rep. of Ireland)	Jun 4	Jun 3
Holiday (Nothern Irealnd)	Jul 12	Jul 12
Holiday		
(Scotland, Rep. of Ireland)	Aug 6	Aug 5
Late Summer Holiday (UK)	Aug 27	Aug 26
Holiday (Rep. of Ireland)	Oct 29	Oct 28
Holiday (Scotland) - optional	Nov 30	Nov 30
Christmas Day		
(UK, Rep. of Ireland)	Dec 25	Dec 25
Boxing Day (UK)	Dec 26	Dec 26
St Stephen's Day		
(Rep. of Ireland	Dec 26	Dec 26

Other Notable Dates	2018	2019
Twelfth Night	Jan 5	Jan 5
Holocause Memorial Day	Jan 27	Jan 27
Shrove Tuesday	Feb 13	Mar 5
St Valentine's Day	Feb 14	Feb 14
Ash Wednesday	Feb 14	Mar 6
St David's Day (Wales)	Mar 1	Mar 1
Mothering Sunday	Mar 11	Mar 31
Commonwealth Day	Mar 12	Mar 11
St Patrick's Day (Ireland)	Mar 17	Mar 17
First Day of Spring	Mar 20	Mar 20
British Summer Time begins	Mar 25	Mar 31
Maundy Thursday	Mar 29	Apr 18
April Fool's Day	Apr 1	Apr 1
Beggining of the Financial Year	Apr 1	Apr 1
Beggining of the Tax Year	Apr 6	Apr 6
Queen Elizabeth II born 1926	Apr 21	Apr 21
St George's Day (England)	Apr 23	Apr 23
May Day	May 1	May 1
Father's Day	Jun 17	Jun 16

	2018	2019
Longest Day-		
First Day of Summer	Jun 21	Jun 21
Midsummer Day	Jun 24	Jun 24
Armed Forces Day	Jun 30	Jun 29
First Day of Autumn	Sep 23	Sep 23
British Summer Time ends	Oct 28	Oct 27
Halloween	Oct 31	Oct 31
All Saints Day	Nov 1	Nov 1
Bonfire Night/		
Guy Fawkes' Night	Nov 5	Nov 5
Armistice Day	Nov 11	Nov 11
Rememberance Sunday	Nov 11	Nov 10
St Andrew's Day (Scotland)	Nov 30	Nov 30
Shortest Day o		
First Day of Winter	Dec 21	Dec 22
Chrismtas Eve	Dec 24	Dec 24
New Yea's Eve/Hogmanay	Dec 31	Dec 31

UK Charity Events/ Awareness Days		
RSPB Big Garden Birdwatch	Jan 27-29	Jan 26-28
Raynaud's Awareness Month	Feb	Feb
Fairtrade Fortnight begins	Feb 26	Feb 25
Marie Curie Great Daffodil Appeal	Mar	Mar
Ovarian Cancer Awareness Month	Mar	Mar
Self-Injury Awareness Day	Mar 1	Mar 1
UK World Book Day	Mar 1	Mar 7
No Smoking Day	Mar 14	Mar 13
Sport Relief	Mar 17-23	-
Red Nose Day	-	Mar 15
National Pet Month	Apr	Apr
Stroke Association -		
Make May Purple	May	May
RNLI Mayday	May	May
SANDS Awareness Month	Jun	Jun
BHF Wear it. Bear it.	Jun 8	Jun 14
Childhood Cancer-		
Awareness Month	Sep	Sep
Epilepsy Action National		
Doodle Day	Sep 21	Sep 20
Macmillan World's Biggest -		
Coffee Morning	Sep 28	Sep 27
Breast Cancer Awareness Month	Oct	Oct
National Poetry Day	Oct 4	Oct 3
National Braille Week begins	Oct 8	Oct 7
Wear it Pink	Oct 19	Oct 18
Pet Diabetes Month	Nov	Nov
BBC Children in Need		
Appeal Night	Nov 16	Tba

NOTABLE DATES

International Awareness Days	2018	2019
World Religion Day	Jan 21	Jan 20
International Women's Day	Mar 8	Mar 8
International Day for the - Elimination of Racial Discrimination	Mar 21	Mar 21
World Water Day	Mar 22	Mar 22
Earth Hour (8:30pm)	Mar 24	Mar 30
World Health Day	Apr 7	Apr 7
World Red Cross and Red Crescent Day	May 8	May 8
World Environment Day	Jun 5	Jun 5
World Refugee Day	Jun 20	Jun 20
World Population Day	Jul 11	Jul 11
International Youth Day	Aug 2	Aug 12
World Humanitarian Day	Aug 9	Aug 19
International Literacy Day	Sep 8	Sep 8
International Day of Peace	Sep 21	Sep 21
World Alzheimer's Day	Sep 21	Sep 21

	2018	2019
World Teacher's Day	Oct 5	Oct 5
World Sight Day	Oct 11	Oct 10
International Day for the - Eradication of Poverty	Oct 17	Oct 17
International Day for the Elimination - of Violence against Women	Nov 25	Nov 25
World Aids Day	Dec1	Dec 1
International Day of Persons - with Disabilities	Dec 3	Dec 3
Human Rights Day	Dec 10	Dec 30

RELIGIOUS FESTIVALS

	2018	2019
Christian - Western		
Epiphany	Jan 6	Jan 6
Ash Wednesday/ First Day of Lent	Feb 14	Mar 6
First Sunday of Lent	Feb 18	Mar 10
Palm Sunday	Mar 25	Apr 14
Good Friday	Mar 30	Apr 19
Easter Sunday	Apr 1	Apr 21
Ascension Day	May 10	May 30
Pentecost	May 20	Jun 9
Trinity Sunday	May 27	Jun 16
First Sunday of Advent	Dec 2	Dec 1
Christmas Day	Dec 25	Dec 25
Christian-Eastern Orthodox		
Christmas- (not greek Orthodox)	Jan 7	Jan 7
Lent Monday	Feb 19	Mar 11
Easter Day	Apr 8	Apr 28
Pentecost	May 27	Jun 16
Hindus		
Holi	Mar 3	Mar 22
Navratri 1st day	Oct 9	Sep 29
Diwali	Nov 7	Oct 27
Chinese		
Lunar New Year (3 days)	Feb 16-18	Feb 5-7
Buddhist		
Parinirvana Day	Feb 15	Feb 15
Wesak (Buddha Day)	May 29	May 18
Dharma Day	Jul 27	Jul 16
Jewish		
Purim	Mar 1	Mar 21
Pesach (Passover) 1st day	Mar 31	Apr 20
Shavuot (Pentecost) 1st day	May 20	Jun 9
Rosh Hashanah (Jewish New year)	Sep 10-11	Sep 30- Oct 1
Yom Kippur (Day of Atonement)	Sep 19	Oct 9
Succot (Tabernacles) 1st day	Sep 24	Oct 14
Hanjukkah 1st day	Dec 3	Dec 23

	2018	2019
Sikh		
Birthday of Guru Gobind Singh Ji	Jan 5	Jan 5
Baisakhi	Apr 14	Apr 14
Martyrdom of Guru Arjan Dev Ji	Jun 16	Jun 16
Birthday of Guru Nanak Dev Ji	Nov 23	Nov 12
Martyrdom of Guru Tegh Bahadur Ji	Nov 24	Nov 24
Islamic		
Lailat al-Isra wa-l-Mi'raj (Prophets Ascension)	Apr 13	Apr 3
Ramadan 1st day	May 16	May 6
Eid al-Fitr 1st day	Jun 15	Jun 4
Eid al-Adha 1st day (Feast of Sacrifice)	Aug 21	Aug 11
Al-Hijra(Islamic New Year)	Sep 11	Aug 31
Ashura	Sep 20	Sep 9
Milad al-Nabi (Prophet's Birthday)	Nov 20	Nov 9
Bahá'í		
Feast of Naw-Rúz	Mar 21	Mar 21
First Day of Ridván	Apr 21	Apr 21
Decleration of the Báb	May 24	May 24
Ascension of Bahá'u'lláh	May 29	May 29
Martyrdom of the Báb	Jul 10	Jul 10
Birth of the Báb	Nov 9	Oct 29
Birth of Bahá'u'lláh	Nov 10	Oct 30

INTERNATIONAL INFORMATION

Country	Capital	Currency	Dialling To	Dialling From	GMT
Australia	Canberra	Dollar	61	0011Δ	+8/+10 ½
Austria	Vienna	Euro	43	00	+1
Belgium	Brussels	Euro	32	00	+1
Canada	Ottawa	Dollar	1	011	-3½ /-8
China	Beijing	Yuan	86	00	+8
Denmark	Copenhagen	Krone	45	00	+1
Finland	Helsinki	Euro	358	00Δ	+2
France	Paris	Euro	33	00Δ	-1
Germany	Berlin	Euro	49	00	+1
Greece	Athens	Euro	30	00	+2
Hong Kong	See China	Dollar	852	001Δ	+8
Hungary	Budapest	Forint	36	00	+1
India	New Delhi	Rupee	91	00	+5 ½
Ireland (Rep.of)	Dublin	Euro	353	00	GMT
Israel	Jeruselem	New Shekel	972	00Δ	+2
Italy	Rome	Euro	39	00	+1
Japan	Tokyo	Yen	81	010Δ	+9
Malaysia	Kuala Lumpur	Ringgit	60	00	+8
Netherlands	Amsterdam	Euro	31	00	+1
New Zealand	Wellington	Dollar	64	00	+12
Nigeria	Abuja	Naira	234	009	+1
Norway	Osio	Krone	47	00	+1
Poland	Warsaw	Zloty	48	00	+1
Portugal	Lisbon	Euro	351	00Δ	GMT
Russian Federation	Moscow	Ruble	7	8‡10	+2/+12
Spain	Madrid	Euro	34	00	+1
Sweden	Stockholm	Krona	46	00	+1
Switzerland	Berne	Franc	41	00	-1
USA	Washington, DC	Dollar	1	011	-5/-10

‡ = wait for dialing tone
Δ = additional/alternative digits for telphone company may be required

Public Holidays (June 2018 - September 2019)

Jun 11; Dec 25, 26; Jan 1,26,28; Apr 19,20,22,25; Jun 10
Aug 15; Oct 26; Nov 1, Dec 8,25,26; Jan 1, 6; Apr 22; May 1,30; Jun 10,20; Aug 15
Jul 21; Aug 15; Nov 1,11; Dec 25; Jan 1; Apr 22; May 1,30; Jun 10; Jul 21; Aug 15
Jul 1 ,2; Aug 6; Sep 3; Oct 8; Nov 11; Dec 25,26; Jan 1; Apr 19,22; May 20; Jul 1; Aug 5; Sep 2
Jun 18, Sep 24; Oct 1,2,3,4,5,6,7, Jan 1; Feb 4,5,6,7,8,9,10 ; Apr 5; May 1; Jun 7; Sep 13
Jun 5; Dec 25,26; Jan 1; Apr 18,19,21,22; May 17,30; Jun 5,9,10
Jun 23*; Nov 3*; Dec 6,25,26; Jan 1,6; Apr 19,21,22; May 1,30; Jun 9,22
Jul 14; Aug 15; Nov 1,11; Dec 25; Jan 1; Apr 22; May 1,8,30; Jun 10; Jul 14; Aug 15
Oct 3; Dec 25,26; Jan 1, Apr 19, 22; May 1,30; Jun 10
Aug 15; Oct 29; Dec 25,26; Jan 1,6; Mar 11,25; Apr 26,28,29; May 1; Jun 16,17; Aug 15
Jun 18; Jul 1,2; Sep 25; Oct 1, 17; Dec 25,26; Jan 1; Feb 5,6,7; Apr 5,19,20,22; May 1,12,13; Jun 7; Jul 1, Sep 14
Aug 20; Oct 23; Nov 1; Dec 25,26; Jan 1; Mar 15; Apr 19,22; May 1; Jun 10; Aug 20
Jun 15; Aug 15,22; Oct 2, 19; Dec 25; Jan 26; Apr 19; Jun 5; Aug 12,15
Jun 4; Aug 6; Oct 29; Dec 25,26; Jan 1; Mar 17; Apr 22; May 6; Jun 3; Aug 5
Sep 10,11,19,24; Oct 1; Apr 20,26; May 9; Jun 9; Sep 30
Jun 2; Aug 15; Nov 1; Dec 8,25,26; Jan 1,6; Apr 21,22,25; May 1; Jun 2; Aug 15
Jul 16; Aug 11; Sep 17,23,24; Oct 8; Nov 3,23; Dec 23,24; Jan 1,14; Feb 11; Mar 21; Apr 29; May 3,4,5,6; Jul 15; Aug 11,12; Sep 16,23
Jun 15,16; Jul 28; Aug 22,31; Sep 11,16,17; Nov 6,20, Dec 25; Jan 1; Feb 5,6; May 1,19,20; Jun 5,6; Jul 27, Aug 11,12,31; Sep 1,2,16
Dec 25,26; Jan 1; Apr 21,22,27; May 30; Jun 9,10
Jun 4; Oct 22; Dec 25,26; Jan 1,2; Fen 6; Apr 19,22,25; Jun 3
Jun 15,16; Aug 21,22; Oct 1; Nov 20, Dec 25,26; Jan 1; Apr 19,22; May 1,29; Jun 4,5; Aug 11,12
Dec 25,26; Jan 1; Apr 18,19,21,22; May 1,17,30; Jun 9,10
Aug 15; Nov 1,11; Dec 25,26; Jan 1,6; Apr 21,22; May 1,3; Jun 9,20; Aug 15
Jun 10; Aug 15; Oct 5; Nov 1; Dec 1,8,25; Jan 1; Apr 19,21,25; May 1; Jun 10,20; Aug 15
Jun 12; Nov 4,5; Dec 31; Jan 1,2,3,4,7,8; Feb 23,25; Mar 8; May 1,9; Jun 12
Aug 15; Oct 12; Nov 1; Dec 6,8,25; Jan 1,6; Apr 18,19; May 1; Aug 15
Jun 6,23; Nov 3; Dec 25,26; Jan 1,6; Apr 19,21,22; May 1,30; Jun 6,9,22
Aug 1; Dec 25,26; Jan 1, Apr 19,22; May 30, Jun 10; Aug 1
Jul 4; Sep 3; Oct 8; Nov 11,22; Dec 25; Jan 1, 21; Feb 18; May 27; Jul 4; Sep 2

CONTENTS

CONFIRMED PEAKY BLINDERS

OF THE PEAKY CLASS

PEAKY CLASS - LATER RACECOURSE VILLAINS

Date: / / /

Jack the Ripper was an un identified serial killer active in the largely impoverished areas in and around the White chapel, a place of poverty and crime, district of London in 1888.

In both criminal case files and contemporay journalistic accounts, the slaughterer was called the White Chapel Murderer and Leather Apron.

Attacks ascribed to Jack the Ripper typically involved female 'prostitutes'. Though with this being said some were not.

Mary Ann Nicholas

On the 31st of August, 1888, the horrifically mutilated body of a woman was discovered in a gateway in Buck's Row, White Chapel. Later that day, she was identified as Mary Ann Nicholas. Or "polly".

She had seperated from her husband and five children in 1880, and

Date: / / /

there after her life became a downward spiral, blighted by poverty and alcholism.

Many ignorant people asked her current family and companions if she were a prostitute. She were not.

Date: / / /

Henry Lightfoot

On December 3rd, 1895, twenty-one–year-old Lightfoot was one of the first men to be actually called a Peaky Blinder.

Following his assault on police officers and other members of the public the court bench pronounced he was "Evidently a 'peaky blinder' of a dangerous type".

Henry Lighfoot was handed a 6 month prison sentence.

The incorrigible Lightfoot continued to offend. The photo taken at the Lock-up Birmingham, in 1904 following his arrest for stealing pork, resulted in yet another period of his life in prison, this time 15 months hard labour followed by 2 years police supervision.

32448 1824 40

NAME Hy Lightfoot Card 427

BORN 1874 HEIGHT 5ft 10

HAIR dk brown EYES brown

COMP. fresh Moulder

DATE 27.1.04

OFFENCE Stg Pork.

RESULT 15 mths + 2 yrs Sup.

MARKS: Sailor & barrel fr lt farm. Scars on lt elbow. Card 427

P 240
G 424
664

714
1100

840

Date: / / /

OUT'S

RENT	595 -	NIBLE (m)	24 -
GAS/ELEC	150 -	ROBLOX	5 - ?
COUNCIL TAX	75 -	APPLE	1 -
CAR	190 -	NEXT	10 - ?
CAR —	150 -	AMAZON M	4 -
INSURANCE	43 - !	BIKE	60 - -
LOAN	281 -		
CAR TAX	14 -		1940
CAR TAX —	12 -		210
GIRL'S SAVING	10 -		2150
BRIER PHONE	30 -		210
PET'S	36 - ?		
WATER	46 -	TOTAL	1824
BUS PASS	50 -		1714
TV	14 -		
REG'S PHONE	31 -	IN	140 -
VIRGIN	28 -		600 -
TAZ	6 - ?		1200 -
PEYTON	10 - ?		1940
AMAZON	8 -		
NETFLIX	10 -		2180
BANK	27 - ?		- 1824
INK	4 -		0326

Date: / / /

LOOK UP RSPCA VET'S

CHANGE P SAVING ✓

PAY OFF NEXT £23

SET UP STANDING ORDER'S
FOR SHOPPING MONEY ✓

46

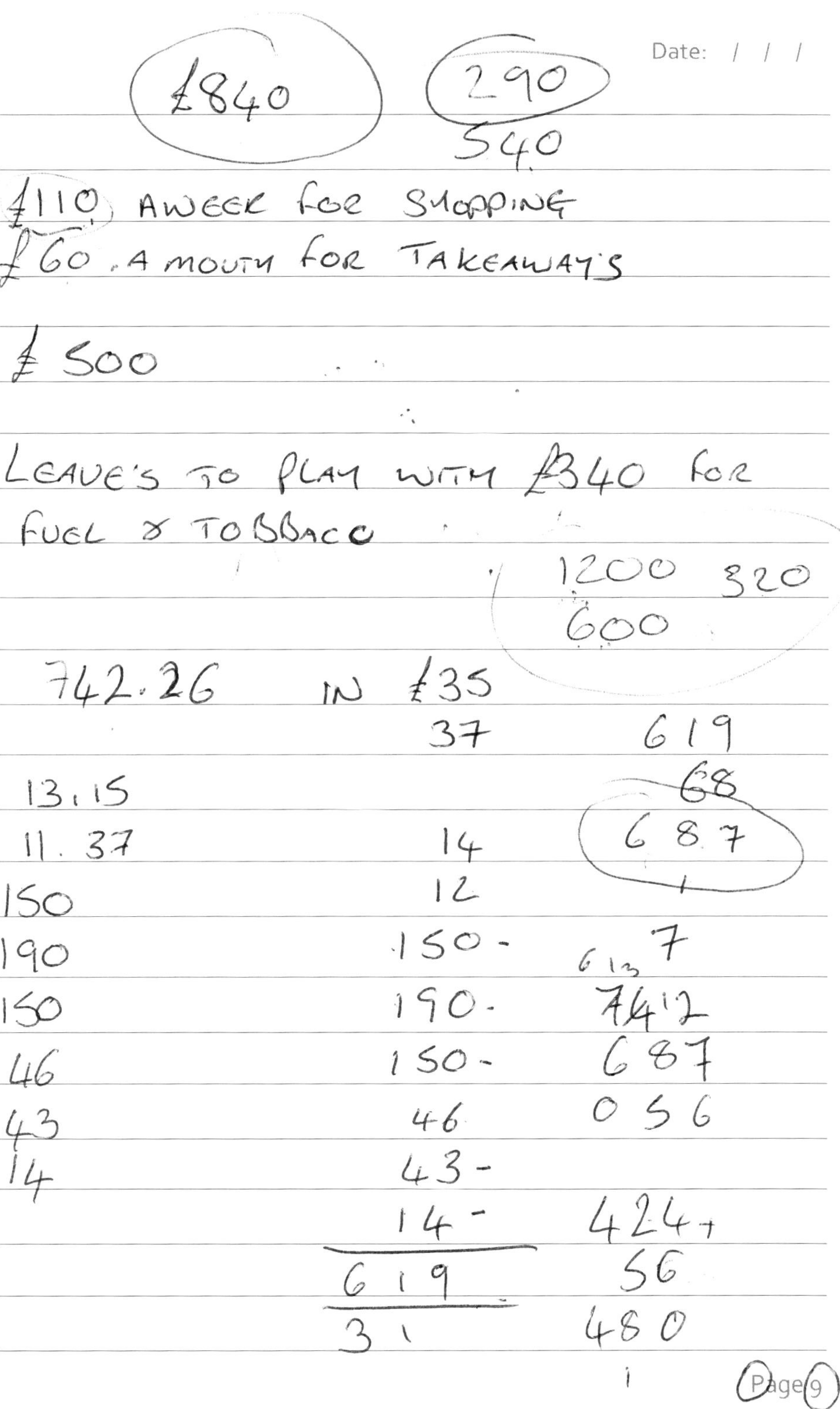
Date: / / /

£840 290
540

£110 A WEEK FOR SHOPPING
£60 A MOUTH FOR TAKEAWAY'S

£500

LEAVE'S TO PLAY WITH £340 FOR
FUEL & TOBBACO

1200 320
600

742.26 IN £35
37 619

13.15 68
11.37 14 687
150 12
190 150- 7
150 190- 742
46 150- 687
43 46 056
14 43-
14- 424+
619 56
31 480

Date: / / /

Date: / / /

Dec

8TH 1200
16TH 600
148 } WEEKLY } TOTAL AMOUNT
140 } " " } PER MONTH

2088

800 1400
1400
1400
200
8TH 1200
13TH

1800
1300

Date: / / /

April 11TH - 17TH -1

MAY 28TH - 3RD

July 23RD - 29

Date: / / /

9 hr's @ £18:74 per week for 9 week's

84 hr's @ £18:74 = 1.57416 - 32.5%

With wage's £ 1730.00

George Fowler

The headline "15 years Penal for 'Peaky Blinders'" appeared in the Gloucester Echo on 14th December 1901, following the fatal assault on PC Charles Philip Gunter on Staniforth Street, Birmingham.

George Fowler was convicted along with two others, however as the judge could not confirm who was ultimately responsible they were subsequently convicted of manslaughter instead of the original charge of murder, and escaped the death penalty.

This sketch was sent to the West Midlands Police Museum by his granddaughter; it was drawn by George Fowler and sent to his future wife whilst in prison.

After he was released before his full term, it is said that he became a reformed character.

Date: / / /

Date: / / /

Date: / / /

Date: / / /

Nicholas Gray

After being court marshalled for striking a senior officer in the Royal Navy in 1895 at the age of 20, Gray's life descended into a life of crime, with convictions for stealing, burglary, warehouse breaking and drunkenness.

When arrested in 1907, his name was recorded in this case as Henry Nicholas Gray, aged 32, and photographed at the Lock-up, Birmingham, for the theft of a coat; he was sentenced to 6 months & 6 months imprisonment (concurrent). Nicholas Gray lived in Allison Street, Birmingham, which is adjacent to Digbeth Police Station, and most likely had a close association in gang crime with his brother in law, Joseph Stevens, another of the confirmed Peaky Blinders.

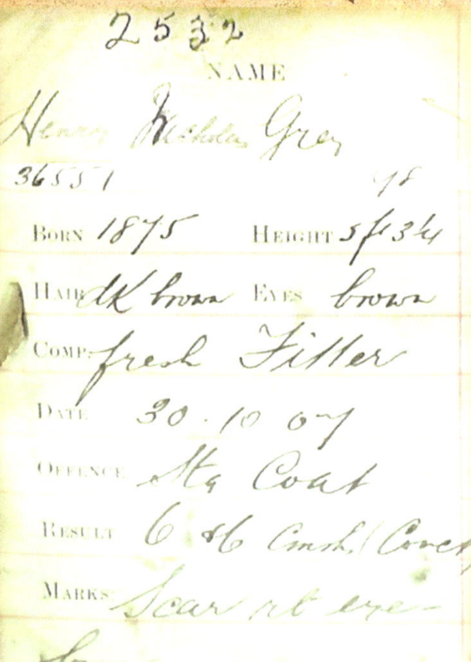

2532

NAME

Henry Nicholas Grey

36551 18

BORN 1875 HEIGHT 5f 3¾

HAIR dk brown EYES brown

COMP. fresh Fitter

DATE 30.10.07

OFFENCE Stg Coat

RESULT 6 & 6 Cmn. (Conct)

MARKS Scar rt eye-brow

Date: / / /

Date: / / /

Date: / / /

Date: / / /

Date: / / /

Joseph Stevens

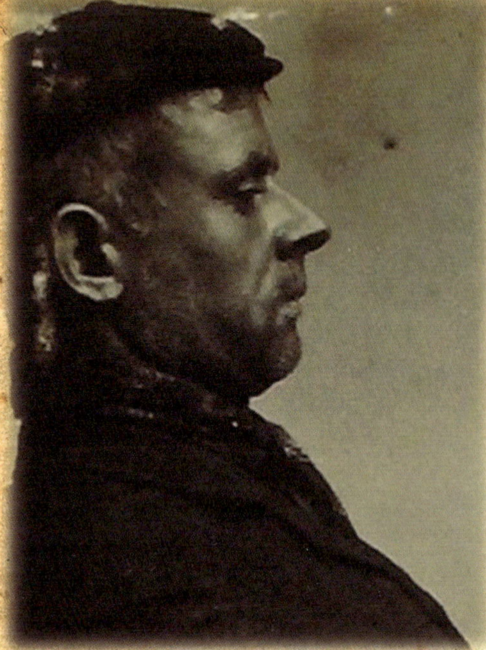

Brother-in-law of Nicholas Gray, Stevens would see many periods of his life behind bars.

The first recorded spell being at Portland Prison at the age of 32, recorded from the 1901 census.

Stevens was considered a violent character after assaulting a police constable, he ran up convictions for burglary, stealing, and deserting a warehouse with clothes.

When he was arrested for house breaking in 1907, and photographed at the Lock-up in Birmingham, he received a sentence of 9 calendar months hard labour and 2 years police supervision.

At one time he lived on Bradford Street, close to the police station on the corner of Alcester Street and Bradford Street.

The census of 1911 records Joseph Stevens back in prison, this time serving time at Stafford prison.

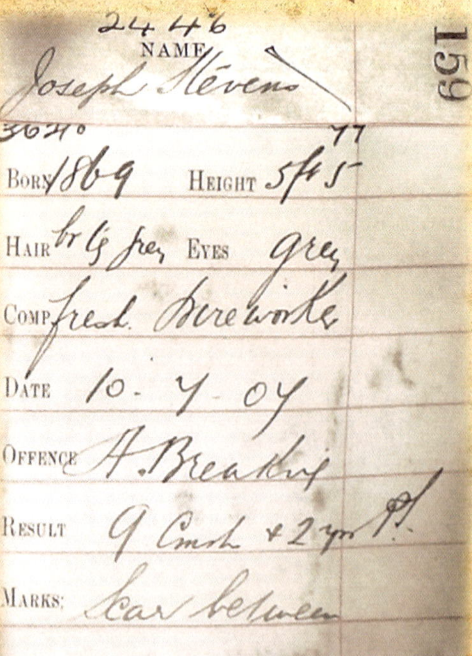

2446 159

NAME Joseph Stevens

Born 1869 Height 5ft 5

Hair br [illegible] grey Eyes grey

Comp fresh [illegible]

Date 10-7-07

Offence H. Breaking

Result 9 Cm & 2 yrs P.S.

Marks: Scar between

Date: / / /

Date: / / /

Date: / / /

John Wallace

Wallace certainly carried the sartorial style of dress akin to those of the "Peaky Class", with his peaky cap and scarf tightly tied around his neck with a neckerchief place in the pocket of his jacket.

Before the camera at the Lock-up in Birmingham, Wallace places his hand across his chest. It could be as per the historic practice of holding hands in front of the body for mugshots, to highlight if the individual is missing any fingers, however it is strange that he only does this with one arm.

Following his arrest at 21 years of age in 1904 he received a hefty 15 months in prison for stealing money followed by 2 years supervision.

PEAKY FACTS 1

"Of The Peaky Class" was a term used by judges to describe "Scallies" in Birmingham during the last decades of the 19th century. A scally being a roguish self-assured young person typically a man, who is boisterous disruptive, or irresponsible.

33431 1684 42

NAME John Wallace

BORN 1883 HEIGHT 5 " 4½

HAIR Sandy EYES Grey

COMP. Fresh

DATE 15 Aug 04

OFFENCE Stg Money

RESULT 15.15.15 Mons concur 2.2.2 yrs sup

MARKS: Scar right cheek near temple

Date: / / /

Date: / / /

Date: / / /

Date: / / /

Date: / / /

Date: / / /

Date: / / /

Date: / / /

Date: / / /

~~SQIDWARD~~

SU

SQUIDWARD

John Joseph Redall

With his hair short at the sides with a fringe deftly swept off his forehead, a scarf neatly wrapped around his neck, the photo image of seventeen-year-old Redall in 1904, certainly portrayed self assurance.

At his court appearance for the malicious wounding of Charles Jolly, with an accomplice, the Birmingham Recorder commented on the liberal use of buckled belts by Peaky Blinders.

Redall was subsequently sentenced to 6 months hard labour.
Prison sentences that included "hard labour" were meted out to the more violent crimes and in some cases house breaking (burglary).

32834 1904 10

NAME John Jos Reddall

BORN 1887 HEIGHT 5-6

HAIR Lt Brown EYES Brown

COMP. Pale Jeweller

DATE 27th January 1904

OFFENCE Wounding

RESULT 6. Cal. Months

MARKS: 2 Hearts on right forearm

Date: / / /

Date: / /

Date: / / /

Date: / / /

Date: / / /

Date: / / /

Date: / / /

Date: / / /

Date: / / /

Ernest Bayles

In 1904 a seemingly relaxed nineteen-year-old Ernest Bayles stares into the police camera at the Lock-up in Birmingham.

Sporting a stylish two piece tweed suit, neatly tied neck scarf and a chequered style peaky cap pinned down low over his forehead.

He would soon be serving two months imprisonment for the mere theft of a bicycle.

33402 NAME 42
Ernest Bayles

BORN 1885 HEIGHT 5' 3½
HAIR L' Bro EYES Grey
COMP. Fresh Barman
DATE 13th October 1904
OFFENCE Stg Bicycle
RESULT 2 Months
MARKS: Mole right cheek near nose.

1450

PEAKY FACTS 2

By the mid 1890's the term "Peaky Blinder" is interchangeable for a particular type of criminality that included minor thefts to violent assaults, not specifically to any one street gang in Birmingham.
The term is reported to have come from the use of Peak Caps pinned down low over the forehead.

Date: / / /

Date: / / /

Date: / / /

Date: / / /

Date: / / /

Date: / / /

Date: / / /

Date: / / /

Frederick Fowler

Twenty-five-year-old Frederick Fowler's charge photo from 1904 certainly portrayed the look of a ruffian.

He was a thief, burglar and later convicted of uttering (circulating) counterfeit coins.

He received 5 months imprisonment for the house breaking conviction of 1904.

Frederick was the older brother of "Peaky Blinder" George Fowler, convicted in 1901 for the manslaughter of PC Charles Philip Gunter.

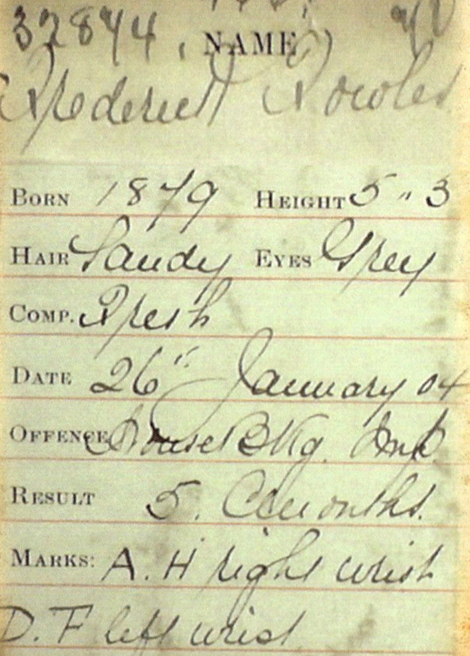

32844, NAME

Frederick Fowler

BORN 1879 HEIGHT 5" 3

HAIR Sandy EYES Grey

COMP. Fresh

DATE 26th January 04

OFFENCE House Brkg.

RESULT 5 Months.

MARKS: A. H right wrist D. F left wrist

Date: / / /

Date: / / /

Date: / / /

Joseph Ellis

The camera image from the Lock-up presents an angelic looking seventeen-year-old, sporting the attire of a "Peaky".

At the turn of the century any type of petty crime could result in a hefty sentence and the start of a spiral into a life of criminality.

Ellis's offence of stealing cigarettes in 1904 resulted in 21 days imprisonment.
He was convicted of multiple thefts thereafter.

33394 NAME 4/1
Joseph Ellis
BORN 1887 HEIGHT 5' 1
HAIR Brown EYES Grey
COMP. Fresh
DATE 21 June 1904
OFFENCE Stg Cigarettes
RESULT 21 days
MARKS: Female front of right forearm, Cross bones & skull left forearm
1664

PEAKY FACTS 3

The term "Peaky Blinder" was first used in a newspaper report on Saturday March 23rd, 1890, to describe a specific gang from the Small Heath area of Birmingham who committed a "Murderous Assault" on George Eastwood. The injury to George's head was so bad that it necessitated the operation of "trepanning" – the drilling of a hole into his head at the Queens Hospital in Bath Row.

Date: / / /

Date: / / /

Date: / / /

Date: / / /

Date: / / /

Date: / / /

Date: / / /

Date: / / /

Date: / / /

Henry Fowler

The camera captures "Baby-Face" Henry at 19 years of aged when charged with the stealing of a bicycle in 1904 from which he would serve one month in prison.

Like a number of "Peakies" he would soon experience the horror of trench warfare at the outbreak of World War One.

He survived being buried alive at the battle of the Somme in 1916.

Claiming that he was unable to speak following his ordeal he was discharged on full pension.

However he would soon fall back upon harder times after his pension was withdrawn when he was caught singing in a Scottish music hall.

33403 NAME 42
Henry Fowler

BORN 1885 HEIGHT 5' 2½
HAIR L' Bro EYES Grey
COMP. Pale & Barman
DATE 13th October 1904
OFFENCE S/g & Bicycle
RESULT 1 month
MARKS: Round scar right chest near side.

* 1449

Date: / / /

Date: / / /

Date: / / /

Date: / / /

Date: / / /

Date: / / /

Charles Belcher

With his neckerchief neatly tied around his neck, peaky cap tipped over his forehead casting a shadow across his eyes, thirty-eight-years old Charles certainly exemplified the style of a more mature looking peaky.

However the judges of the time dealt harsh sentences to this "class" of criminal.

Charles was sentenced to 12 months imprisonment for stealing a bag from a traveller at a railway station, a popular target for pickpockets and thieves, where crowds and ultimately their victims were in abundance.

PEAKY FACTS 4

No contemporary newspaper reports can be found to support the notion that razor blades were sewn into the peak caps so that they could be used as weapons. The disposable safety blade was not patented until 1901 in America, and therefore considered a luxury item at the beginning of the 20th century until they were made more readily available. The idea of the razor blades sown into the caps has its roots in John Douglas's novel "A Walk Down Summer Lane".

NAME
33484 Charles Belcher

BORN 1866 HEIGHT 5.5

HAIR Bro G.G EYES Grey

COMP. Fresh

DATE 24 Oct 04

OFFENCE Stg Bag Rly Stn

RESULT 12 Mons 2 yrs Sup

MARKS: Blind right eye 2 dots back of left forearm

1914

Date: / / /

Date: / / /

Date: / / /

Date: / / /

Date: / / /

Date: / / /

Date: / / /

Date: / / /

Date: / / /

Walter Hobday

Walter was caught with the tools of the trade in his possession at a house break-in in Birmingham.

The judge passed a more lenient sentence than his partner in crime who received 5 years imprisonment as for whatever reason he was deemed a more dangerous villain than Walter.

He did however receive 6 months imprisonment that could quite as easily been passed as a term of penal servitude, that being a term that included hard labour, dreaded by prisoners.

32924 NAME 41
Walter Hobday

BORN 1871 HEIGHT 5-2
HAIR L. Brown EYES Grey
COMP. Fresh
DATE 24th January 1904
OFFENCE H. Brkg Implements
RESULT 6 Months
MARKS: Dot back of each forearm.

1405

Date: / / /

Date: / / /

Date: / / /

Date: / / /

John Southgate

Wearing a smart looking two piece suit that appears oversized for his frame, a white collared shirt and tie and peaky cap, you are drawn into the dark piercing eyes of Southgate.

In the early hours of the morning the occupants of a house in Pershore Road Birmingham would be woken up and come face to face with Southgate and his accomplice as they burglarised their house.

He was subsequently arrested for the burglary and sentenced to 3 months imprisonment.

33408 NAME 42
John Southgate

BORN 1884 HEIGHT 5 " 3
HAIR Brown EYES Brown
COMP. Pale
DATE 5th July 1904
OFFENCE Burglary
RESULT 3. Months.
MARKS: Anchor Love 2 hearts back of left forearm.

1684

PEAKY FACTS 5

During the 1890's and through the early first years of the 1900's "Peaky Blinders" were frequently reported in the newspapers throughout the country.
The most serious conviction being the fatal assault on PC Charles Philip Gunter, reported in the Gloucester Echo on the 14th December 1901.
In that same year the Cheltenham Chronicle reported the near fatal stabbing of PC Bennett at a separate incident at another location in Birmingham.

Date: / / /

Date: / / /

Date: / / /

Date: / / /

Date: / / /

Date: / / /

Date: / / /

Date: / / /

Date: / / /

Thomas Gilbert

For some reason when taking his custody photograph at the Lock-up in Birminghamin 1904, the decision was made to take two pictures, one wearing his peaked cap and another without.

The weary looking Thomas looks older than his 38 years as he stares at the camera lens.

He would soon face 3 months imprisonment for using false pretences to extract money and food from the poor class of people he preyed upon.

This one legged criminal sometimes pleaded for subscriptions for his cork leg.

NAME 33422 M2 Thomas Gilbert		NAME	
Born 1866	Height 5' 4	Born 1866	Height 5' 4
Hair Brown	Eyes	Hair Brown	Eyes
Comp. Fishmonger		Comp. Fishmonger	
Date 18 October 1904		Date 18 October 1904	
Offence False Pretences		Offence False Pretences	
Result 3 Months		Result 3 Months	
Marks: 2nd 3rd & 4th left finger missing. Right leg off near knee		Marks: 2nd 3rd & 4th left finger missing. & Right leg off near knee	

1452

Date: / / /

Date: / / /

Date: / / /

Date: / / /

Date: / / /

Date: / / /

Date: / / /

Walter Brown

Sharp eyed thirty-six-year-old Walter, with just one top button fastened on his tailored jacket covering a white collared shirt and his peaky cap snugly pulled down over his forehead was a repeat offender.

At his arrest for obtaining items using false pretences he had been convicted no less than 4 times over the previous 4 year period for felony.

Felony is a term used to differentiate crimes deemed more serious than crimes classed as "misdemeanours", he was subsequently sentenced to 9 months imprisonment.

PEAKY FACTS 6

Towards the end of the 19th century the reference in newspaper reports to Peaky Blinders had but almost disappeared. However the plundering of race courses, local and further afield, during the last decades of the 19th century, by the loose collection of small gangs from Birmingham, would gain increased notoriety through into the 20th century. The infamy of the small gangs would soon collectively become known as the "Brummagem Boys".

33643 NAME 4/2
Walter Brown

BORN 1868 HEIGHT 5" 6
HAIR Brown EYES Grey
COMP. Fresh
DATE 1 Nov 04
OFFENCE False Pretences
RESULT 9 Months
MARKS:
Nil

1933

Date: / / /

Date: / / /

Date: / / /

Date: / / /

Date: / / /

Roblox IDs

6917155909
6681840651
6708444383
9042248317
8964762256
11999179563
6913550990

Date: / / /

Date: / / /

Stephen McNickle

With his peaky style cap pulled down low over his forehead and spotted scarf tied neatly around his neck, unlike many others whose image is captured by the camera at the Lock-up in 1904, the rest of his attire presents a scruffy looking McNickle, with a dirty well worn jacket again only fastened by the top button.

The 8 months sentence passed that year for house breaking in no way re-formed McNickle, he was again convicted for theft and assault prior to World War One.

After serving and surviving two tours of France during that Great War, enemy gunshot wounds would result in the amputation of one of his arms, most likely inhibiting his life of crime.

33904 NAME 72
Stephen McNickle

BORN 1879 HEIGHT 5' 4½
HAIR Black EYES Brown
COMP. Sallow, Metal Polisher
DATE 29 Oct '04 Sess.
OFFENCE Shopbreaking
RESULT 8 Months
MARKS: Female & cross flag left arm, Female Louisa right arm, Female on left forearm.

1451

PEAKY FACTS 7

By 1905 a Birmingham born felon had progressed to leading the Brummagem's. Billy Kimber was clever and charismatic, and through a combination of brain and brawn as well as the credentials of a natural born leader, he ensured his gang fully exploited the spoils from racetrack extortion. Forming alliances with other gangs for control of the many racecourse venues across the country, they would come up against many other of the feared gangs who were fighting for ultimate supremacy.

Date: / / /

Date: / / /

Date: / / /

Joseph Witton

Between 1900 and 1907 Joseph Witton had received five convictions for theft, four for drunkenness, two for assault; and one each for drunk and disorderly, loitering and indecent language.

When arrested for larceny from the person in 1906 and photographed after his arrest at the Lock-up in Birmingham, he was sentenced to 3 years penal servitude and 2 years police supervision.

He was released early as he was handed a four year term in prison and a "flogging" for robbery with violence in 1908.

During the First World War 1914-1918 he served in the Worcestershire Regiment and was posted to France and Gallipoli.

During that time he deserted twice and was finally discharged in 1918 for house breaking in Birmingha

Witton was one of 28 from Billy Kimbers "Birmingham Gang" arrested following the "Epsom Road Battle", on June 2, 1921.

The gang had fought with bookmakers from Leeds after the Epsom races, who they had believed they were switching sides to the Sabinis.

Witton was sentenced to 3 years hard labour.

NAME
Joseph Witton

BORN 1877 HEIGHT 5f 4½

HAIR Lt brown EYES hazel

COMP. fresh Barber

DATE 31. 10. 06

OFFENCE Lar Person

RESULT 3 years PS & 2 yrs PS

MARKS:

2335

Date: / / /

Date: / / /

Date: / / /

Date: / / /

Date: / / /

Henry Tuckey

The custody photograph taken at the Lock-up in 1906 presents a typical peaky portrait of thirty-one-year old Henry Tuckey following his arrest for stealing a bicycle, along with his younger brother, Edward Tuckey.

They would both receive the same punishment, being imprisoned for 15 months penal servitude and 15 months imprisonment to run concurrently.

Both brothers were arrested following the "Epsom Road Battle", on June 2, 1921.

At this time both brothers also shared the same occupation as bricklayers along with their gang member antics.

Now forty-six-years old, he was sentenced to eighteen months hard labour.

NAME

Henry Tuckey

34886
Born 1875 Height 5ft 9¾
Hair brown Eyes grey
Comp. fresh Bricklayer
Date 25.1.06
Offence Stg Bicycle
Result 15 & 15 Cmth (Conct)
Marks: Scar forearm (rt)

2150

Date: / / /

Date: / / /

Date: / / /

Date: / / /

Date: / / /

Date: / / /

Date: / / /

Edward Tuckey

Younger brother of Henry Tuckey, he was arrested along with his older brother for stealing a bicycle.

The custody photograph shows twenty-two-year-old Edward Tuckey with his peaky cap perched on top of a very carefully styled mop of hair.

Despite being the younger of the two brothers he received the same sentence of 15 months penal servitude and 15 months imprisonment to run concurrently.

It seems that he would follow very closely in his older brother's footsteps, he was arrested along with his brother Henry Tuckey following the "Epsom Road Battle", on June 2, 1921, when 28 members of the "Birmingham Gang" fought with bookmaker's from Leeds.

Edward Tuckey was sentenced to fifteen months hard labour, 3 months less than his older brother Henry.

2122
NAME
Edwd. Tuckey
34885

Born 1884 Height 5ft 6½
Hair brown Eyes brown
Comp. fresh Bricklayer
Date
Offence 25. 1. 06
Result Stg Bicycle.
Marks: 15 & 15 Cush (Covet)
Butterfly front rt farm

Date: / / /

Date: / / /

Date: / / /

Date: / / /

Date: / / /

Date: / / /

Date: / / /

Date: / / /

Date: / / /

Ernest Mack

When Ernest Mack was photographed in 1907 at the age of thirty-six he was discharged for allegedly passing three counterfeit coins in the Golden Fleece Inn, Edgbaston Street, Birmingham, on the basis that it couldn't be proven that he knew about the coins.

This villain would later become a known member of Billy Kimber's Birmingham gang that targeted racecourse meetings across the country.

Now at the age of 50, Mack was jailed for a term of 3 months for demanding money from bookmakers with threats at a race meeting at Epsom in 1921, during the notorious year of gang "turf wars".

2422

NAME

Ernest Mack

36515 74

BORN 1871 HEIGHT 5ft 9

HAIR brown EYES grey

COMP. fresh Hawke

DATE 29.10.07

OFFENCE Base coin

RESULT Dis Jr.

MARKS: Cut scar left side of ch

Date: / / /

Date: / / /

Date: / / /

Thomas McDonald

4496
NAME
Thos McDonald
36381 7F
BORN 1883 HEIGHT Lt brown
HAIR Lt brown EYES grey
COMP. fresh Labourer.
DATE 28·10·07
OFFENCE Bodily harm
RESULT 9 Cmths & 6 Cmths (Consec)
MARKS Peacock bk rt fore. flower bk left fore

When just 10 years of age, McDonald felt the rod of the birch afterhe was caught stealing a loaf of bread, the consequence of going hungry.

His journey into adolescence would see him face a number of convictions for obstruction and illegal gaming.

In 1907, at the age of twenty-four it would be the face of a violent criminal captured by the police camera at the Lock-up in Birmingham.

McDonald had been arrested for causing grievous bodily harm to William Tooley and sentenced to 9 months hard labour.

He was also handed a 6 month prison sentence to be served consecutively for assaulting a police officer.

By the time he had turned forty-years he had become known as a notorious street fighter and bully among the Midland race gangs of the time.

Thomas McDonald was viciously attacked by a number of men from a rival gang when the race course wars broke out again in 1925, he did however recover from this attack, to be left with a scar running from ear to mouth.

His journey into adolescence would see him face a number of convictio

Date: / / /

Date: / / /

Date: / / /

Moses Kimberley

The 1907 custody photograph of Moses Kimberley shows a clean cut twenty-two-year-old with his hair neatly parted down the middle; he had been arrested for satchel snatching.

Moses Kimberley received 8 months imprisonment for this offence, but later in life became embroiled in violent skirmishes as a Birmingham gang member.

On June 23rd, 1925, the 'Yorkshire Post and Leeds Intelligence' reported the attack on Thomas McDonald, claiming that Moses Kimberley was one of the attackers who carried out the severe wounding of McDonald, leaving him dazed outside a Birmingham public house, after receiving several blows to the head and serious wounds from razor slashes to his face.

NAME
Moses Kimberley
36610
BORN 1885 – HEIGHT 5ft 8 75
HAIR brown EYES grey
COMP. fresh. Fruiterer
DATE 28.11.07 (Ass)
OFFENCE Satchel snatching
RESULT 8 Cmths
MARKS: Scar left cheek
Dot bk rt wrist

2481

Date: / / /

Stephen	Rachael

Date: / / /

RENT	750		
EBENE GATE	110	IVA	
NETFLIX	14		
WATER	19		
CAR IN	32		
COUNCIL TAX	127		
KLARNA	12		
GAS	42		
SKY	35		
PHONE'S	64		
BIKE IN	13		
BIKE	60		360 x 4
CAR	150		1200
AMAZON	8		240
O2	18		1440
O2	19		
[illegible]			
	1473		560 x 4
			2240 -
			1473
			767

The Lock-up Birmingham - where members of the Peaky Blinder gang were held in police cells before facing trial.

First published 2018

Published by Mapseeker Archive Publishing Ltd, 9 Jordan Way, Aldridge, Walsall, WS9 8SB
Tel: +44(0)1922 458288 / +44(0) 7947107248

Printed by Think Digital Books Ltd, Unit 15, Bridgwater Court, Oldmixon Crescent, Weston super Mare, North Somerset, BS24 9AY Tel: +44(0)1934 620400

British Library Cataloguing in Publication Data.
A catalogue record for this book is available from the British Library.

The Victorian Lock-up, built in 1891, was created to house prisoners from across Birmingham between arrest and their appearance in court. It is steeped in history and is where the real Peaky Blinders were held before facing trial. It is a grade II listed building and is now being converted into the new home of the West Midlands Police Museum.

ISBN: 978-1-84491-878-2

THURSDAY 14TH

17.28

TIME OF ACCIDENT

ASK IF THE PAYMENT'S STOP